Anonymous

The Hymns, Anthems and Tunes, with the Ode Used at the Magdalen Chapel

Set for the organ, piano forte, voice, German-flute or guitar

Anonymous

The Hymns, Anthems and Tunes, with the Ode Used at the Magdalen Chapel
Set for the organ, piano forte, voice, German-flute or guitar

ISBN/EAN: 9783744795999

Printed in Europe, USA, Canada, Australia, Japan

Cover: Foto ©Thomas Meinert / pixelio.de

More available books at **www.hansebooks.com**

THE

HYMNS ANTHEMS and TUNES

with the ODE used at the

MAGDALEN CHAPEL

Set for the

ORGAN

HARPSICHORD, VOICE

GERMAN-FLUTE

or

GUITAR

Price 2^{s}

LONDON

Printed for HENRY THOROWGOOD under the Royal Exc.

HYMN I

For the Morning

A-wake my Soul, and with the Sun, Thy daily Stage of Du-ty run: Shake off dull Sloth, and ear- - -ly rife, To pay thy Morning Sa-cri-fice.

2

Redeem thy mif-fpent Moments paft
And live this Day, as if 'twere laft:
Thy Talents to improve take care;
For the great Day thy felf prepare.

3

Let all thy converfe be fincere,
Thy confcience, as the Noon-Day clear;
For God's all-feeing Eye furveys
Thy fecret Thoughts, thy Works, and Ways.

4

Wake, and lift up thy felf my Heart,
And with the Angels bear thy part;
Who, all Night long, unwearied fing
High Glory to th'eternal King.

I wake, I wake, ye heavenly Choir,
May your Devotion me infpire:
That I, like you, my Age may fpend;
Like you, may on my God attend.

6

May I, like you, in God delight;
Have all Day long my God in fight;
Perform, like you, my Maker's will;
Oh! may I never more do ill.

7

Glory to Thee, who fafe haft kept,
And haft refrefh'd me whilft I flept;
Grant, Lord, when I from Death fhall wake,
I may of endlefs Life partake.

8

Lord, I my Vows to thee renew;
Scatter my Sins as morning Dew;
Guard my firft fpring of Thought and Will,
And with thy felf my Spirit fill.

9

Direct, Controul, Suggeft this Day,
All I defign, or do, or fay;
That all my Pow'rs, with all their Might,
In thy fole Glory may unite.

10

Praife God, from whom all Bleffings flow;
Praife him, all Creatures here below;
Praife him above, angelic Hoft:
Praife Father, Son, and Holy Ghoft.

HYMN II

The spacious Firmament on high With all the blue etherial Sky

And spangled Heav'ns, a shining Frame, Their great Original proclaim.

2
Th'unwearied Sun from Day to Day,
Does his Creator's pow'r difplay,
And publifhes to ev'ry Land,
The Work of an Almighty hand.

3
Soon as the ev'ning Shades prevail,
The Moon takes up the wond'rous Tale,
And Nightly to the lift'ning Earth
Repeats the Story of her birth:

4
Whilft all the Stars that round her burn,
And all the Planets in their turn,
Confirm the Tycings as they roll,
And fpread the Truth from Pole to Pole.

5
What though in folemn Silence all
Move round this dark terreftial Ball?
What though not real Voice nor Sound
Amid their radiant Orbs be found?

6
In reafon's Ear they all rejoice,
And utter forth a glorious Voice;
For ever Singing as they fhine,
"The Hand that made us is Divine."

The Lord my Pasture shall prepare, And feed me with a Shepherd's Care; His
Presence shall my Wants supply, And guard me with a watchfull Eye: My
Noon-Day Walks he shall attend, And all my Midnight Hours defend.

2

When in the fultry Glebe I faint,
Or on the thirfty Mountain pant,
To fertile Vales and dewy Meads
My weary wandering Steps he leads,
Where peaceful Rivers, foft and flow,
Amid the verdant Landfkip flow.

3

Though in the paths of Death I tread;
With gloomy Horrors over-fpread,
My ftedfaft Heart fhall fear no Ill,
For thou, O Lord, art with me ftill:
Thy friendly Crook fhall give me Aid,
And guide me thro' the dreadful Shade.

4

Though in a bare and rugged Way,
Through devious lonely Wilds I ftray,
Thy Bounty fhall my Pains beguile,
The barren Wildernefs fhall fmile,
With fudden Greens and Herbage crown'd,
And Streams fhall murmur all around.

HYMN IV

The Chriftian's Hope

When rifing from the Bed of Death, O'er-whelm'd with Guilt and Fear;

I fee my Maker, face to face; O how fhall I appear!

2

If yet, while Pardon may be found,
And Mercy may be fought,
My Heart with inward Horror fhrinks,
And trembles at the Thought.

3

When thou, O Lord, fhalt ftand difclofd
In Majefty fevere,
And fit in Judgment on my Soul,
O how fhall I appear!

4

But thou haft told the troubled Mind,
Who does her Sins lament;
The timely Tribute of her Tears
Shall endlefs Woe prevent.

5

Then fee the Sorrow of my Heart,
E'er yet it be too late;
And hear my Saviour's dying Groans
To give thefe Sorrows weight.

6

For never fhall my Soul defpair
Her Pardon to procure,
Who knows thy only Son has dy'd,
To make her Pardon fure.

HYMN V

On Gratitude

When all thy Mercies, O my God, My rising Soul surveys; Tran
-- sported with the View, I'm lost In Wonder, Love, and Praise.

2

O how shall Words with equal warmth,
The Gratitude declare,
That glows within my ravish'd Heart!
But thou canst read it there.

3

Thy Providence my Life sustain'd,
And all my Wants redreft,
When in the silent Womb I lay,
And hung upon the Breast.

4

To all my weak complaints and cries
Thy Mercy lent an Ear,
Ere yet my feeble Thoughts had learnt,
To form themselves in Pray'r.

5

Unnumber'd Comforts to my Soul,
Thy tender Care bestow'd,
Before my Infant Heart conceiv'd,
From whence those Comforts flow'd.

6

Thro' hidden dangers, toils, and deaths,
It gently clear'd my Way,
And thro' the pleasing Snares of Vice,
More to be fear'd than they.

7

When worn by sickness, oft haft thou
With Health renew'd my Face:
And when in Sin and Sorrow shrunk,
Reviv'd my Soul with Grace.

8

Ten thousand thousand precious Gifts
My daily Thanks employ;
Nor is the least a chearful Heart,
That tastes those Gifts with Joy.

9

Through ev'ry Period of my Life
Thy goodness I'll pursue;
And after Death in distant Worlds
The glorious Theme renew.

10

When Nature fails, and Day and Night
Divide thy Works no more;
My ever-grateful Heart, O Lord,
Thy Mercy shall adore:

11

Through all Eternity to Thee
A joyful Song I'll raise;
For oh! Eternity's too short
To utter all thy Praise.

HYMN VI

On the Excellency of the BIBLE

Great God, with Wonder and with Praife, On all thy Works I look:

But ftill thy Wifdom, Pow'r, and Grace, Shine brighter in thy Book.

2

The Stars that in their Courfes roll,
Have much Inftruction given;
But thy good Word informs my Soul
How I may foar to Heaven.

3

The Fields provide me Food, & fhew
The goodnefs of the Lord;
But Fruits of Life and Glory grow
In thy moft holy Word.

4

Here are my choiceft Treafures hid,
Here my beft Comfort lies;
Here my Defires are fatiffy'd,
And hence my Hopes arife.

5

Lord, make me underftand thy Law,
Shew what my Faults have been;
And from thy Gofpel let me draw
Pardon for all my Sin.

6

Here would I learn how Chrift has dy'd
To fave my Soul from Hell:
Not all the Books on Earth befide
Such heav'nly Wonders tell.

7

Then let me love my Bible more,
And take a frefh Delight,
By Day to read thefe Wonders o'er,
And meditate by Night.

HYMN VII

On the Sabbath

Lord of the Sabbath, hear our Vows On this thy day, in this thy houſe; Ac-cept, as grateful Sacrifice, The Songs which from thy Servants rise.

2

Thine early Sabbaths Lord we love
But there's a nobler Reſt above:
To that our lab'ring Souls aſpire
With ardent Pangs of ſtrong Deſire.

3

No more Fatigue, no more Diſtreſs,
Nor Sin nor Hell ſhall reach the Place:
No Groans to mingle with the Songs,
Reſounding from immortal Tongues.

4

No rude alarms of raging Foes;
No cares to break the long Repoſe;
No midnight Shade, no clouded Sun,
But Sacred, High, Eternal Noon.

5

O long expected Day! begin:
Dawn on theſe realms of Woe and Sin:
Fain would we leave this weary Road,
And ſleep in Death, to reſt with God.

HYMN VIII

On the Sacrament

My God and is thy Table spread. And does thy Cup with love o'er-flow.

Thither be all thy Children led, And let them all thy sweetness know.

2
Hail sacred Feast, which Jesus makes!
Rich banquet of his Flesh and Blood!
Thrice happy He, who here partakes
That sacred Stream, that heav'nly Food.

3
Why are its dainties all in vain
Before unwilling Hearts display'd.
Was not for You the Victim slain.
Are You forbid the Children's bread.

4
O let thy Table honour'd be,
And furnish'd well with joyful Guests;
And may each Soul salvation see,
That here its sacred Pledges tastes.

5
Let Crouds approach with Hearts prepard;
With Hearts inflam'd let all attend:
Nor, when we leave our Father's board,
The Pleasure or the Profit end.

6
Receive thy dying Churches, Lord,
And bid our drooping Graces live,
And more than energy afford,
A Saviour's blood alone can give.

HYMN IX

On the Sacrament

And are we now brought near to God, Who once at diftance ftood.

And to effect this glorious Change, Did Jefus fhed His Blood!

2

Oh! for a Song of ardent Praife
To bear our Souls above!
Whut fhould allay our lively hope,
Or damp our flaming love.

3

Draw us O Lord, with quick'ning Grace,
And bring us yet more near;
Here we may fee thy Glories fhine
And tafte thy Mercies here.

4

Oh! may that love, which fpread thy board,
Difpofe us for the Feaft;
May Faith behold a fmiling God
Thro' Jefu's bleeding Breaft.

5

Fir'd with the View, our Souls fhall rife
In fuch a Scene as this;
And view the happy Moment near,
That fhall compleat our Blifs.

HYMN X

On Chriftmas Day

High let us fwell our tuneful Notes And join th'angelic Throng

For Angels no fuch Love have known T'awake a chearful Song—

— — T'awake a chearful Song.

2

Good will to finful Men is fhewn,
And peace on Earth is giv'n;
For lo! th'incarnate Saviour comes
With meffages from Heav'n.

3

Juftice and Grace, with fweet Accord,
His rifing Beams adorn;
Let Heav'n and Earth in Concert join,
Now fuch a Child is born.

4

Glory to God in higheft ftrains,
In higheft Worlds be paid;
His Glory by our Lips proclaim'd,
And by our Lives difplay'd.

5

When fhall we reach thofe blifsful Realms
Where Chrift exalted Reigns;
And learn of the coleftial Choir,
Their own immortal Strains!

For Easter   by Mr Worgan

Jesus Christ is ris'n to Day, Hal _ _ _ le _ lu _ jah! Our Triumphant Ho _ ly Day, Hal _ _ _ le _ lu _ jah! Who did once up _ on the Cross; Hal _ _ _ le _ lu _ jah! Suf _ fer to re _ deem our loss. Hal _ _ _ le _ lu _ jah.

2

Hymns of Praife then let us fing Hallelujah
Unto Chrift our heav'nly King; Hallelujah
Who endur'd the Crofs and Grave, Hallelujah
Sinners to Redeem and Save, Hallelujah

3

But the Pains which he endur'd, Hallelujah
Our Salvation hath procur'd; Hallelujah
Now above the Sky he's King, Hallelujah
Where the Angels ever Sing. Hallelujah

HYMN XII

On the laft Judgment

[musical notation]

The Day of Wrath, that dreadful Day Shall the whole

World in Afhes lay, As DAVID and the SYBILS fay.

2
What Horror will invade the Mind,
When the ftrict Judge, who would be kind,
Shall have few venial Faults to find?

3
The laft loud Trumpet's wond'rous found,
Shall thro' the rending Tombs rebound,
And wake the Nations under Ground.

4
Nature and Death fhall, with furprize,
Behold the pale Offender rife,
And view the Judge with confcious Eyes.

5
Then fhall with univerfal dread,
The facred, myftic Book be read,
To try the Living and the Dead.

6
The Judge afcends his awful Throne,
He makes each fecret Sin be known,
And all with Shame confefs their own.

7
Oh! then what int'reft fhall I make,
To fave my laft important Stake,
When the moft Juft have caufe to quake!

Thou mighty, formidable King,
Thou Mercy's unexhaufted fpring,
Some comfortable Pity bring.

9

Forget not what my Ranfom coft,
Nor let my dear-bought Soul be loft,
In Storms of guilty Terror toft.

10

Thou, who for me did'ft feel fuch Pain,
Whofe precious Blood the Crofs did ftain,
Let not thofe Agonies be vain.

11

Thou, whom avenging Pow'rs obey,
Cancel my Debt, too great to pay,
Before the fad accounting Day.

12

Surrounded with amazing Fears,
Whofe load my Soul with Anguifh bears,
I figh, I weep, accept my Tears.

13

Thou, who were mov'd with MARY'S grief,
And by abfolving of the Thief,
Haft giv'n me Hope, now give Relief.

14

Reject not my unworthy Pray'r:
Preferve me from that dang'rous Snare
Which Death and gaping Hell prepare.

15

Give my exalted Soul a Place,
Among thy chofen right-hand Race,
The Sons of God, and Heirs of Grace.

16

From that infatiable Abyfs,
Where Flames devour, and Serpents hifs,
Promote me to thy Seat of blifs.

17

Proftrate my contrite Heart I rend,
My God, my Father, and my Friend,
Do not forfake me in my End.

18

Well may they curfe their fecond Breath,
Who rife to a reviving Death:
Thou great Creator of mankind,
Let guilty Man compaffion find!

HYMN XIII

For Whitsunday

Creator Spirit by whose Aid, The Worlds foundations first were laid;

Come visit ev'ry pious Mind Come pour thy Joys on Human kind.

2

From Sin and Sorrow set us free,
And make thy Temples worthy thee:
Illumine our dull darken'd sight,
Thou Source of uncreated Light.

3

Thrice holy Fount, thrice holy Fire,
Our hearts with heav'nly love inspire:
Come, and thy sacred Unction bring,
To Sanctify us while we sing.

4

Plenteous of Grace, descend from high,
Rich in thy seven-fold Energy!
Thou strength of his Almighty hand,
Whose Pow'r, does heav'n & earth commnd

5

Proceeding Spirit, our defence,
Who dost the gift of Tongues dispence:
Refine and purge our earthly parts;
But oh! inflame and fire our hearts!

6

Our frailties help; our Vice controul;
Submit the Senses to the Soul;
Feeble, alas! we are, and frail;
Let not the World or Flesh prevail!

7

Chace from our Minds th'infernal Foe,
And Peace, the Fruit of love bestow:
And left our Feet should step astray,
Protect and guide us in the Way!

8

Make us eternal Truths receive,
And practice all that we believe:
Give us thy felf, that we may fee
The Father and the Son by Thee!

9

Immortal Honours, endless Fame
Attend th'Almighty Father's name;
The Saviour Son be glorified
Who for loft Man's redemption died:

10

And equal Adoration be,
Creator Spirit, paid to Thee:
" Come, visit ev'ry pious Mind; —
" Come, pour thy Joys on Human kind!

For a Faft Day

Great God of Hofts attend our Pray'r, And make the britifh

Ifles thy Care; To thee we raife our fuppliant Cries, When angry

Nations round us rife.

2
Fain would they tread our Glory down,
And in the Duft defile our Crown,
Deluge our Houfes, with our Blood,
And burn the Temples of our God.

3
But 'midft the Thunder of their Rage,
We thy Protection would engage;
O raife thy faving Arm on high,
And bring renew'd deliv'rance nigh.

4
May Britain as one Man be led,
To make the Lord her fear and dread;
Our Souls no other Fears fhall know,
Tho' Earth were leagu'd with Hell below.

5
Give ear, ye Countries from afar,
Ye proud affociate Nations, hear,
While fix'd on him who rules the Sky,
Our Hearts your threat'ned War defy.

6
Ye People gird yourfelves in vain,
Your fcatter'd Force unite again;
Again fhall all that Force be broke,
When God, with us, fhall deal y Stroke.

7
Now he records our humble Tears,
With ardent Vows for future Years,
And deftines for approching Days,
Victorious fhouts & fongs of Praife.

8
Emanuel's land fhall fafe remain,
Bleft with its Saviour's gentle reign;
Till ev'ry hoftile rumour ceafe,
In the fair Realms of perfect Peace.

For the Lord's Day

This is the Day, the Lord's own Day, A Day of Ho_ly Rest:

O teach our Souls to rest from Sin, That Rest will please Thee best.

This is the Day, the Day, O Lord, On which Thou didst a__rise;

For Sinners having made thy self A sinless Sa_cri_fice.

2

Thou, thou alone, redeemed hast
Our Souls from deadly thrall;
With no less price than thine own Blood,
The Purchase of us all.
Hadst Thou not dy'd We had not liv'd,
But dy'd eternally;
We'll live to him who dy'd for us,
And praise his Name on high.

3

Thou, Lord, didſt die, and riſe again,
And didſt aſcend on high,
That we, poor Sinners, loſt and dead,
Might live eternally.
Thy Blood was ſhed inſtead of ours
Thy Soul our Guilt did bear;
Thou tookſt our Sins gavſt us thy ſelf;
Thy Love's beyond compare.

4

Welcome and dear unto my Soul
Is thy moſt Holy day:
May I th'eternal Sabbath keep
With God my Strength and Stay!
I come, I wait, I hear, I pray;
Thy Footſteps, Lord, I frace:
I joy to think this is the Way
To ſee my Saviour's Face:

5

Theſe are my preparation Days,
And when my Soul is dreſt,
Theſe Sabbaths ſhall deliver me
To mine eternal Reſt.
To Father, Son, and Holy Ghoſt,
All Glory be therefore;
As in beginning was, is now,
And ſhall be evermore.

HYMN XVI

On the Paffion

From whence thefe dire portends around, That Earth and Heav'n a-

_ _ maze. Wherefore do Earthquakes cleave the Ground. Why hides the

Sun his Rays?

2

Not thus did Sinai's trembling head
With facred Horror nod,
Beneath the dark Pavilion fpread
Of the defcending God!

3

Thou Earth thy loweft centre fhake,
With Jefu fympathize!
Thou Sun, as Hell's deep gloom be black,
'Tis thy Creator dies!

4

What tongue the Tortures can declare
Of this vindictive Hour?
Wrath he alone had will to fhare,
As he alone had Pow'r!

5

See, ftreaming from the fatal Tree,
His all-atoning Blood!
Is this the infinite? —'Tis he!
My Saviour and my God!

6

For me thefe pangs his Soul affail,
For me the Death is borne!
My Sin gave fharpnefs to the Nail,
And pointed ev'ry Thorn.

7

Let Sin no more my Soul enflave;
Break, Lord, the Tyrants chain;
O fave me, whom thou cam'ft to fave,
Nor Bleed nor Die in vain!

On the New Year

God of my Life, thy conftant Care With Bleffings crowns the op'ning Year, This guilty Life doft thou prolong; And wake a-new mine annual Song.

2

How many precious Souls are fled
To the vaft Regions of the Dead,
Since from this Day the changing Sun
Thro' his laft yearly Period run.

3

We yet furvive; but who can fay,
Or thro' the Year, or Month, or Day,
" I will retain this vital Breath;
" Thus far at leaft in league with Death".

4

That breath is thine, eternal God;
'Tis thine to fix my Soul's abode
It holds its life from thee alone,
On Earth, or in the World unknown.

5

To thee our Spirits we refign;
Make them, and own them ftill as thine;
So fhall they fmile fecure from Fear,
Tho' Death fhould blaft the rifing Year.

6

Thy Children, eager to be gone,
Bid Time's impetuous Tide roll on,
And land them on that blooming Shore,
Where Years and Death are known no more.

HYMN XVIII

For Midnight

My God now I from Sleep a-wake, The fole Pof-fef-fion
of me take; From midnight Terrors me fecure, And guard my
Heart from Thoughts impure.

2

Bleft Angels, while we filent lie,
You Hallelujah's fing on high:
You joyful Hymn the ever bleft;
Before the Throne, and never reft.

3

I with your Choir Celeftial join,
In off'ring up a Hymn divine:
With you in Heav'n I hope to dwell;
And bid the Night and World farewell.

4

My Soul, when I fhake off this duft,
Lord, in thy Arms I will entruft:
O make me thy peculiar Care,
Some manfion for my Soul prepare.

5

Give me a Place at thy Saints feet,
Or fome fall'n Angel's vacant feat:
I'll ftrive to Sing as loud as they,
Who fit above in brighter Day.

6

O may I always ready ſtand,
With my Lamp burning in my Hand:
May I in ſight of Heav'n rejoice,
When e'er I hear the Bride-groom's voice.

7

All praiſe to Thee, in light array'd,
Who light thy dwelling-place haſt made:
A boundleſs Ocean of bright beams,
From thy all glorious God-head ſtreams.

8

The Sun in its meridian height,
Is very darkneſs in thy ſight:
My Soul O lighten and enflame,
With thought and love of thy great Name.

9

Bleſs'd Jeſus, thou, on Heav'n intent,
Whole Nights haſt in devotion ſpent;
But I, frail Creature ſoon am tir'd,
And all my Zeal is ſoon expir'd.

10

My Soul, how canſt thou weary grow
Of antedating Bliſs below:
In ſacred Hymns and Heav'nly Love,
Which will eternal be above.

11

Shine on me, Lord new life impart
Freſh ardours kindle in my Heart:
One ray of thy all quick'ning light,
Diſpels the Sloth and Clouds of Night.

12

Lord, leſt the Tempter me ſurprize,
Watch over thine own ſacrifice:
All looſe, all idle Thoughts caſt out,
And make my very Dreams devout.

13

Praiſe God, from whom all Bleſſings flow,
Praiſe him, all Creatures here below:
Praiſe him, above angelic Hoſt:
Praiſe Father, Son, and Holy Ghoſt.

HYMN XIX

Thanks to God

All glorious God what Hymns of Praife, Shall our tran-
-fported Voices raife: What flaming Love and Zeal is due, While
Heav'n ftands o-pen to our View.

2

Once we were fall'n, and oh how low!
Juft on the brink of endlefs Woe
Doom'd to the Heritage in Hell;
Where Sinners in deep darknefs dwell.

3

But lo, a Ray of chearful light,
Scatters the horrid Shades of Night:
Lo, what triumphant Grace is fhewn,
To Souls impov'rifh'd and undone!

4

Far, far beyond thefe mortal Shores
A bright Inheritance is ours:
Where Saints in light our coming wait,
To fhare their holy blifs-ful State.

5

If ready dreft for Heav'n we fhine,
Thine are the Robes, the Crown is thine:
May endlefs Years their courfe prolong,
While, "Thine the Praife", is all our Song.

Public Thanksgiving

Salvation doth to God belong; His Pow'r and Grace shall be our Song;

His hand hath dealt a deadly blow, And Terror strikes the haughty Foe.

2

Praise to the Lord, who bows his Ear,
Propitious to his People's Pray'r;
And, tho' deliv'rance long delay,
Answers in his well-chosen Day.

3

O, may thy Grace our Land engage,
(Rescu'd from fierce tyrannic Rage)
The Tribute of its Love to bring
To Thee, our Saviour, and our King.

4

Our Temples guarded from the Flame,
Shall echo thy triumphant Name;
And ev'ry peaceful private Home,
To Thee a Temple shall become.

5

Still be it our supreme Delight
To walk as in thy honour'd Sight:
Still in thy Precepts and thy Fear
To life's last Hour to persevere.

HYMN XXI

On The unknown World

Hark, my gay Friend, that solemn toll, Speaks the departure of a Soul: 'Tis gone, that's all, we know not where, Or how th'un_body'd Soul does fare.

2
In that mysterious World none knows,
But God alone to whom it goes;
To whom departed Souls return,
To take their doom, to smile or mourn.

3
Oh! by what glimm'ring light we view,
That unknown World were hast'ning to!
God has lock'd up the mystic Page,
And curtain'd darkness round y Stage!

4
Wise Heav'n, to render search perplext,
Has drawn 'twixt this World & the next
A dark impenetrable Screen,
All behind which is yet unseen!

5
We talk of Heav'n we talk of Hell;
But what they mean, no Tongue can tell!
Heav'n is the Realm where Angels are,
And Hell the Chaos of despair.

6
But what these awful Words imply,
None of us know, before we die!
Wether we will or no, we must
Take the succeeding World on trust.

7
This Hour perhaps our Friend is well
The next, we hear his passing bell!
He dies! and then, for aught we see,
Ceases at once to breathe and be.

8
Thus launch'd from Life's ambiguous Shore
Ingulph'd in Death, appears no more;
Then, undirected to repair
To distant Worlds, we know not where.

Swift flies the Soul; perhaps 'tis gone
A thoufand Leagues beyond the Sun;
Or twice ten Thoufand more thrice told,
E're the forfaken Clay is cold.

10
And yet who knows, if Friends we lov'd,
Tho' dead may be fo far remov'd?
Only this veil of Flefh between,
Perhaps they watch us, tho' unfeen.

11
Whilft we, their lofs lamenting, fay,
"They're out of hearing far away;"
Guardians to us, perhaps they're near,
Conceal'd in vehicles of Air.

12
And yet no notices they give,
Nor tell us where or how they live;
Though confcious whilft with us below,
How much themfelves defir'd to know.

13
As if bound up by folemn fate,
To keep this fecret of their State;
To tell their Joys or Pains to none,
That Man may live by Faith alone.

14
Well, let my Sov'reign, if he pleafe,
Lock up his marvellous Decrees;
Why fhould I wifh him to reveal
What he thinks proper to conceal.

15
It is enough that I believe,
Heav'ns brighter far than we concieve;
And they who make it all their care,
To ferve God here fhall fee him there.

16
But, oh! what Worlds fhall I furvey
The moment that I leave this clay.
How fudden the Surprize, how new!
Let it, my God, be happy too!

The With

In vain the dufky Night retires, And fullen Shadows fly: In

vain the Morn with purple light, Adorns the eaftern Sky.

2

In vain the gaudy rifing Sun,
The wide Horizon gilds;
Comes glitt'ring o'er the filverftreams,
And chears the dewy Fields.

3

In vain difpenfing vernal fweets,
The morning Breezes play;
In vain the Birds with chearful fongs,
Salute the new-born Day.

4

In vain, unlefs my Saviour's Face
Thefe gloomy Clouds controul,
And diffipate the fullen Shades
That prefs my drooping Soul.

5

Oh! vifit then thy Servant, Lord,
With Favour from on high,
Arife, my bright immortal Sun,
And all thefe Shades will die.

6

Lord, when fhall I behold thy Face,
All radiant and ferene,
Without thofe envious dufky Clouds
That make a Veil between.

7

When fhall that long expected Day
Of facred Vifion be,
When my impatient Soul fhall make
A near approach to Thee.

On Charity

Did sweeter sounds a-dorn my flowing Tongue, Than e-ver

Man pronounc'd or An-gels sung:

2
Had I all knowledge human & divine,
ThatThought can reach,orSciencecanda fine
3 birth
And had I power to give that knowledge
In all the Speeches of the babling Earth.
4 spire
Did Shadrach's zeal my glowing breast in
To weary Tortures & rejoice in Fire.
5
Or had I faith like that which Israel saw,
When Moses gave them miracles & law.
6
Yet gracious Charity indulgent Guest,
Were not thy Pow'r exerted in thy Breast.
7 Pray'r
Those speeches would send up unheeded
That scorn of life would be but wild despair
8 Voice
A Cymbal's sound were better than my
My Faith were form my Eloquence were noise
9
Charity, Decent,Modest,Easy, Kind,
Softens the high,& rears y abject Mind.

10 guide
Knows with just reins,& gentle hand to
Betwixt vile Shame,& arbitrary Pride.
11
Not soon provok'd, she easily forgives,
And much she suffers,as she much believes
12 rives
Soft Peace she brings,wherever she ar
She builds our quiet,as she forms our lives
13 ev'n
Lays the rough Paths of pevish nature
And opens in each heart a little Heav'n.
14 ftow
Each other Gift which God on Man bes
Its proper bound,& due reflection knows
15
To one fix'd purpose dedicate its Pow'r,
And finishing its act;exists no more.
16 crees
Thus in obedience to what Heav'n de-
Knowledge shall fail,& Prophecy shall
17 cease.
But lasting Charity's more ample sway,
Not bound by Time,nor subject to decay.

18
In happy Triumph shall for ever live,
And endless good diffuse,and endless praise recieve.

HYMN XXIV

For the use of the Sick

My God, with grateful Heart I'll raife A daily Altar to thy Praife;

Thy friendly Hand my Courfe directs, Thy watchful Eye my Bed protects.

2
When Dangers, Woes, or Death are nigh,
Paft Mercies teach me where to fly;
The fame almighty Arm can aid,
Now Sicknefs grieves, and Pains invade.

3
To all the various help of Art,
Kindly thy healing Pow'r impart,
Bethosdis bath refus'd to fave
Unlefs an Angel blefs'd the Wave.

4
All med'cines act by thy decree,
Recieve commiffion all from Thee:
And not a Plant which fpreads the Plains,
But teems with health, when Heav'n ordains.

5
Clay and Siloam's Pool we find,
At Heav'n's command reftor'd the Blind,
Hence Jordan's Waters once were feen
To wafh a Syrian Leper clean.

6
But grant me nobler Favours ftill,
Grant me to know and do thy Will;
Purge my foul Soul from ev'ry Stain,
And fave me from eternal Pain.

7
Can fuch a Wretch for Pardon fue!
My Crimes, my Crimes arife in view,
Arreft my trembling Tongue in Pray'r,
And pour the Horrors of defpair.

8
But oh! regard my contrite Sighs,
My tortur'd Breaft, my ftreaming Eyes;
To me thy boundlefs Love extend,
My God, my Father, and my Friend.

9
Thefe lovely Names I ne'er could plead,
Had not thy Son vouchfaf'd to bleed;
His blood procures for Adam's race
Admittance to the Throne of Grace.

10
When Vice hath fhot its poifon'd Dart,
And confcious Guilt corrodes the Heart;
His Blood is all-fufficient found,
To draw the Shaft, & heal the Wound.

11
What Arrows pierce fo deep as Sin?
What Venom gives fuch Pain within?
Thou great Phyfician of the Soul,
Rebuke my Pangs, and make me whole.

12
Oh! if I truft thy fov'reign Skill,
With deep fubmiffion to thy Will;
Sicknefs and Death fhall both agree,
To bring me, Lord, at laft to Thee.

HYMN XXV

For the Evening

Glory to Thee my God this Night, For all the Bleſſings of the Light,

Keep me, O keep me, King of Kings, Under thy own Almighty Wings.

2

Forgive me Lord, for thy dear Son,
The Ills that I this Day have done;
That with the World, my-ſelf, and Thee,
I, ere I ſleep, at Peace may be.

3

Teach me to live, that I may dread,
The Grave as little as my Bed;
Teach me to die, that ſo I may
With Joy behold the Judgment Day.

4

O may my Soul on Thee repoſe,
And with ſweet Sleep mine eye-lids cloſe;
Sleep, that may me more active make
To ſerve my God when I awake.

5

When reſtleſs in the Night I lie,
My Soul with heav'nly Thoughts ſupply:
Let no ill Dreams diſturb my Reſt,
No pow'rs of Darkneſs me moleſt!

6

Let my bleſt Guardian, while I Sleep,
His watchful Station near me keep;
My Heart with Love Celeſtial fill,
And guard from the approach of ill.

7

Lord, let my Soul for ever ſhare,
The Bliſs of thy Paternal care;
'Tis heav'n on earth, 'tis heav'n above,
To ſee thy Face, and ſing thy Love.

8

Shou'd Death itſelf my ſleep invade
Why ſhou'd I be of Death afraid?
Protected by thy ſaving Arm,
Tho' he may ſtrike, he cannot harm.

9

For Death is Life, and labour reſt
If with thy gracious Preſence bleſ
Then welcome Sleep, or Death to m
I'm ſtill ſecure, for ſtill with Thee!

10

Praiſe God, from whom all Bleſſings flow;
Praiſe him, all Creatures here below:
Praiſe him above, angelic Hoſt:
Praiſe Father, Son, and Holy Ghoſt.

ANTHEM I

Praife ye the Lord, for he is good For his Mercy endureth for

e _ _ _ ver. Give praife un_to the God of Gods, For his Mer_

_ _cy en_du_reth for e_ _ver. Give praife unto the Lord of Lords

For his Mer_cy en _du_reth for e_ _ver. Who only doth great

wond'rous Works, For his Mer_cy en_du_reth for e_ver.

ANTHEM II

Let us with a gladfome Mind, Praife the Lord for he is kind,

For his Mercies ftill en-dure, E—ver faithful e—ver fure. :S:

Solo
Let us blaze his Name abroad, For of Gods he is the God.

Slow
Chorus
For his Mercies ftill endure, E—ver faithful e—ver fure. :S:

Solo	Who did the fixt Earth ordain,
	To rife from the watry Plain.
Cho:	For his Mercies &c
Solo	Who ordain'd the glorious Sun,
	All the Day his Courfe to run.
Cho:	For his Mercies &c
Solo	And the Moon to fhine by Night,
	Mid her fpangled Sifters bright.
Cho:	For his Mercies &c
Solo	He hath with a piteous Eye,
	Seen us in our Mifery. Da Capo

Tune. to the firft PSALM

The Man is bleft that hath not lent, To wicked Men his Ear:

6   56   5 6 6   #

Nor led his Life as Sinners do, Nor fat in Scorner's chair.

6 6   6   6 6
   5

Tune. to the 8th or 23d PSALM

O God our Lord how wonderful Are thy Works ev'ry where!

6   6 6   6 6   #   6 6   #
5   4   4 5
       3   2

Thy Fame furmounts in Dignity, The higheft Heav'ns that are.

6   6   6 5
       #   #   6 4

Tune. to the 18th PSALM

O God, my Strength and Fortitude, Of force I muft love Thee:

6   6   6

Thou art my Caftle and defence In my ne-cef-fi-ty.

6 6 #   6   6 5
            4 3

Tune. to the 104th PSALM

My Soul praise the Lord Speak good of his Name, O Lord our great

6   6   6   6 56

God, how doft thou appear! So paffing in Glory that great is thy

6   #   6   6 56

Fame: Honour and Majefty in Thee fhine moft clear.

6   6   6
4 ft

Tune. to the 51. PSALM

O Lord con-fi-der my diftrefs, And now with fpeed fome

6   6 6   6 6   6 6

Pi-ty take: My Sins forgive, my Faults re-drefs,   Good

6 6   5   6 6   6   6   6 5
4 #   6   4 3

Lord, for thy great Mercies fake.

to the 121st PSALM

7 Eyes to Sion hill, From whence I do attend, Till succour

6
5   6   6
        4
        3   6   6

d, The mighty God me succour will, Which Heav'n and

6   6   6   5
4♮   5♮   ♯

Earth did frame, And all Things all Things therein name.

6
        6
♯   6   4
            3

he 112th & 127th PSALM

n is blest that God doth fear, And that his law doth love indeed,

♯   ♯   6   6 ♯

n Earth God will up rear, And bless such as from him proceed,

6   6   5   ♮   ♯   5 6   ♯
    4   ♯

fe with riches he will fill, His Righteousness endure shall still.

5   6   5
3
♮   6   ♯   4   ♯
        ♮

THE ODE

Andante
Chorus

Grateful Notes, & numbers bring while Jehovah's praise we sing,

6   6   6   6   6   6   6 5
                                          4 3

Holy Holy Holy Lord   be thy glorious Name ador'd.

6   #   6   6   #7 5 6   6   5
                           3   3 3 3   4   #

Semi Chorus
1ſt Gallery   2d Gallery

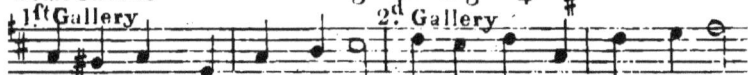

Men on Earth and Saints above Men on Earth and Saints a-bove

Minuetto

Tho' un-wor--thy, Lord thine Ear, our hum---ble

Hal-le--lu--jahs hear, Purer Praise we hope to

Cho.

bring when with Saints we stand and sing.

Siciliana

Lead us to that bliss-full State where thou reign'st su-

--premely great look with Pity from thy Throne & send thy

Ho--ly Spirit down while on Earth ordain'd to ftay

guide our Footfteps in thy Way 'till we come to reign with

Thee and all thy glorious Greatnefs fee   Cho: Vivace

Then with Angels

2ᵈ Gall.   Cho.

we'll a--gain wake a louder louder Strain wake a louder

1ᶠᵗ Gall.

louder Strain There in joyfull Songs of Praife we'll our gratefull

2d Gall.

Voices raife there in joyfull Songs of Praife we'll our gratefull Voices

Semi Cho: 1ft Gall.

raife there no Tongue fhall filent be there all fhall join fweet har_mo-

__ny that thro' Heav'ns all fpacious round thy Praife O God may ever found.

Full Chorus

Lord thy mercies never fail Lord thy mercies never fail Hail. hail. Ce-

__leftial Goodnefs Hail. Hail. Hail. Ce_lef_tial Goodnefs Hail.

These Words go to the
Eleventh Hymn Tune

HYMN XXVI

On Thanksgiving

1
Glory be to God our King, Hal:&c
Thine eternal love we fing:
Thou haft barr'd thine Arm divine,
Wrought Salvation made us thine.Hal:

2
Wand'ring Sheep, how far from home,
Sore bewilder'd, did we roam.
Till the gracious Shepherd came:
Sought and Sav'd:O praife his name.

3
Death, no more we dread thy Sting;
Sin fubdu'd, we joyful fing:
Grave, thy Terrors we defy;
We fhall live; for Chrift did die.

4
Fir'd with Gratitude, we raife
All our Souls to found thy Praife;
Touch each Heart, each Tongue infpire,
Sing we higher, ftill and higher.

5
Down to deepeft Hell depreft,
Jefu refcu'd, raif'd, and bleft;
Open'd Mercy's golden Gate,
Mercy, here who holds her feat.

6
Happy Manfion—ev'ry Voice,
In the bleft retreat rejoice;
Let each Voice united found,
"Be the Walls with gladnefs crown'd."

7
Bleffings, Lord, profufely fhed,
On each Hand, each Heart, each Head;
Who, with gen'rous Pity join,
In the great, the good Defign.

8
Elevate our Souls to Thee;
Thou our Guide and Guardian be;
Worthy, worthy may we prove,
Lord, of fuch diftinguifh'd Love.

9
Bleffing, thankful all our Days
May we Pray. Rejoice, and Praife;
Till the glorious Trump fhall found,
And our raptur'd Hearts rebound.Hal:

These Words go to the
Second Hymn Tune

HYMN XXVII

Againft Lewdnefs

1
Why fhould you let your wand'ring eyes
Entice your Souls to fhameful Sin!
Scandal and Ruin are the Prize
You take fuch fatal Pains to win.

2
This brutal Vice makes reafon blind,
And blots the Name with hateful ftains;
It waftes the Flefh, pollutes the Mind,
And tears the Heart with racking Pains.

3
Let DAVID fpeak with heavy Groans,
How it eftrang'd his Soul from God;
Made him complain of ceafelefs moans,
And fill'd his houfe with Wars & Blood.

4
Let Solomon and Samfon tell,
Their melancholly Stories here;
How bright they fhone, how low they fell.
When Sin's vile Pleafures coft them dear.

5
In Vain you chufe the darkeft Time,
Nor let the Sun behold the Sight;
In Vain you hope to hide your crime,
Behind the Curtains of the Night.

6
The wakeful Stars & midnight Moon
Watch your foul deeds & know your fhame
And Gods own Eye, like beams of Noon
Strikes thro'y fhade, & marks your name.

7
What will ye do when Heav'n enquires
Into thofe Scenes of fecret Sin?
And luft with all it's guilty Fires,
Shall make your Confcience rage within

8
How will you curfe your wanton eyes.
Curfe the lewd partners of your fhame.
When Death, with horrible furprize,
Shews you the Pit of quenchlefs Flame

9
Flee, Sinners, flee th' unlawful Bed,
Left Vengeance fend you down to dwell
In the dark Regions of the Dead,
To feed the fierceft Fire in Hell.

A PRAYER for the Ufe of the
MAGDALEN CHAPEL

Father of Mercies, and God of all Comfort, who haft fent thy Son JESUS CHRIST into the World, to feek and to fave that which was loft, we praife thy Holy Name for the bountiful Provifion made in this Place, for the fpiritual and temporal Wants of miferable Offenders: befeeching Thee fo to difpofe our Hearts by the powerful working of thy Bleffed Spirit, that thro' fincere Repentance and a lively Faith, we may obtain remiffion of our Sins, and all the precious promifes of thy Gofpel. Awaken thofe, who have not yet a due Senfe of their Guilt; and perfect a godly Sorrow, where it is begun. Renew in us whatfoever hath been decayed by the fraud and malice of the Devil, or by our carnal Will and Frailnefs: Preferve us, after efcaping the Pollutions of the World, from being again intangled therein; and keep us in a State of conftant Watchfulnefs and Humility. Forgive, as we do from our Hearts, thofe who have injured us: and grant to all, who have feduced others, or have been feduced themfelves into wickednefs, that they may forfake the evil of their doings and live. Make this Houfe a Bleffing, we pray Thee, to the Souls and Bodies of all its inhabitants; and a glorious Monument of thy Grace, abounding to the chief of Sinners, Strengthen the Hands, direct the Counfels, reward the Labours and the Liberality, of all who are engaged in the Government or Support of it: and increafe the number of thofe, who have a Zeal for thy Glory, and compaffion on the Ignorant, and on them that are out of the Way; that many may be turned from Darknefs to Light, and from the power of Satan unto Thee their God, through the Merits and Mediation of JESUS CHRIST our LORD. Amen.

A MAGDALEN in HER UNIFORM.

A Second Collection

of

PSALMS and HYMNS

Us'd at the

MAGDALEN CHAPEL

The Words by

Dr Watts	Dr Dodd
Dr Doddridge	Mr Dryden

AND

Mr Lockman

The Musick Compos'd by

Dr Arne

{ Mr Willm Selby }
and
{ Mr Adam Smith }

Late Organists of the Chapel

Set for the Organ

HARPSICHORD VOICE

VIOLIN GERMAN FLUTE

AND

GUITTAR
Price 1, 6.

LONDON,
Printed for HENRY THOROWGOOD, at N? 6 North Piazza Royal Ex=
=change.

THE favourable Reception the Magdalen Pſalms and Hymns have met with from the Public, has induced the Publiſher to procure from the late Organiſts of the Chapel, ſome new Tunes (which are occaſionally perform'd there) to the after-mentioned Pſalms and Hymns, which exactly correſpond with the Boards and Books belonging to the Chapel, and never before publiſh'd. He alſo begs Leave to inform them, that the old Edition is to be had (being the only correct one of any publiſh'd) at his Shop, No. 6, North Piazza, *Royal Exchange.*

Where alſo may be had, Six favourite Hymns uſed at the Tabernacles of the Rev. Meſſ. *Whitefield* and *Weſley.* Price 1 s.

I N D E X.

PSALM XIX

The Mufick by
Mr Selby

The fpa_cious fir..ma..ment on high, with all the

blue e..the..rial Sky, And fpang.led Heav'ns a fhin..ing

Frame, their great O...ri..gi...nal pro...claim.

2

Th' unwearied fun from day to day,
Does his Creator's pow'r difplay;
And publifhes to ev'ry land
The work of an almighty Hand.

3

Soon as the ev'ning fhades prevail,
The Moon takes up the wond'rous tale,
And nightly to the lift'ning earth
Repeats the ftory of her birth:

4

Whilft all the ftars that round her burn,
And all the planets in their turn,
Confirm the tidings as they roll,
And fpread the truth from pole to pole

5

What though in folemn filence all
Move round this dark terreftrial ball?
What though nor real voice nor found
Amid their radiant orbs be found?

6

In reafon's ear they all rejoice,
And utter forth a glorious voice;
For ever finging as they fhine,
"The hand that made us is divine."

PSALM XXIII

The Musick by Mr Selby

The

Lord my Pasture shall pre_pare, And feed me with a Shep.herds

care; His Presence shall my

vants sup..ply And guard me with a watch ful Eye:

My noon day walks he shall at..

...tend. And all my Mid..night hours de..fend.

2

When in the fultry glebe I faint,
Or on the thirfly mountain pant.
To fertile vales and dewy meads
My weary wandering fteps he leads,
Where peaceful rivers foft and flow,
Amid the verdant landfkip flow.

3

Though in the paths of death I tread,
With gloomy horrors overfpread,
My ftedfaft heart fhall fear no ill,
For thou O Lord art with me ftill
Thy friendly crook fhall give me aid,
And guide me through the dreadful fhade.

4

Though in a bare and rugged way,
Through devious lonely wilds I ftray,
Thy bounty fhall my pains beguile,
The barren wildernefs fhall fmile,
With fudden greens and herbage crown'd,
And ftreams fhall murmur all around.

HYMN IV

On GRATITUDE the words from the Spectator the Mufick by _Mr. Selby_

When all thy Mer_cies, O my God, My ri_fing

Soul fur_veys, Tranfported with the View, I'm loft In

Won_der Love and Praife.

O how fhall words with equal warmth
  The gratitude declare
That glows within my ravifh'd heart,
  But thou can'ft read it there.

3
Thy providence my life fuftain'd
  And all my wants redreft,
When in the filent womb I lay
  And hung upon the breaft.

4
To all my weak complaints and cries
  Thy mercy lent an ear,
E'er yet my feeble thoughts had learnt
  To form themfelves in prayer.

5
Unnumber'd comforts on my foul
  Thy tender care beftow'd,
Before my infant heart conceiv'd
  From whom thofe comforts flow'd.

6
When worn by ficknefs, oft haft thou
  With health renew'd my face:
And when in fin and forrow funk,
  Reviv'd my foul with grace.

7
Ten thoufand thoufand precious gifts
  My daily thanks employ,
Nor is the leaft a chearful heart
  That taftes thofe gifts with Joy.

8
Through ev'ry period of my life
  Thy goodnefs I'll purfue,
And after death in diftant worlds
  The glorious theme renew.

9
When nature fails and day and night
  Divide thy works no more,
My ever greatful heart O Lord
  Thy mercy fhall adore.

HYMN V

On the Excellency of the *BIBLE* by *Dr Watts*   The Mufick by M' Selby

Great God with

Wonder and with Praife On all thy works I look

But ftill thy wifdom power and Grace Shine brighter in thy Book

The ftars that in their courfes roll,
Have much inftruction given;
But thy good word informs my foul
How I may foar to heaven.

2

Lord make me underftand thy law,
Shew what my faults have been;
And from thy gofpel let me draw
Pardon for all my fin.

3

The fields provide me food, and fhew
The goodnefs of the Lord;
But fruits of life and glory grow
In thy moft holy word.

4

Here are my choiceft treafures hid,
Here my beft comfort lies;
Here my defires are fatisfy'd,
And hence my hopes arife.

5

6

Here would I learn how Chrift has dy'd,
To fave my foul from hell:
Not all the books on earth befide
Such heav'nly wonders tell.

7

Then let me love thy fcriptures more
And with renew'd delight,
By day read all thy wonders o'er,
And meditate by night.

HYMN VI

On the SABBATH by Dr Doddridge   The Musick by Mr Smith

Lord of the Sabbath, hear us pray in this thy House on this thy day Ac-

...cept as gratefull Sacrifice;The songs, which from thy Servants rise.

2

Thine earthly Sabbaths, Lord, we love,
But there's a nobler REST above,
Oh that we might that REST attain
From sin, from sorrow, and from pain.

3

In thy blest kingdom we shall be
From every mortal trouble free,
No groans shall mingle with the songs
Resounding from immortal tongues.

4

No rude alarms of raging foes,
No cares to break the long repose,
No midnight shade no clouded sun,
But sacred high eternal noon.

5

O long expected day begin,
Dawn on these realms of woe and sin,
Fain would we leave this weary road,
To sleep in death and rest with GOD.

HYMN VIII
on CHRISTMAS day
Sung by the Women at the Magdalen Chapel :   set by Mr Adam Smith.

High let us swell our tunefull notes, & join th'Angelic throng for Angels no such love

High let us &c

have known to wake a chearfull song - - - - to wake a chearful song.

2

Good will to sinful men is shewn,
And peace on earth is given,
For lo th'incarnate Saviour comes
With messages from heaven

3

Justice and grace with sweet accord,
His rising beams adorn,
Let heaven and earth in concert Join
" To us a child is born."

4

"Glory to God in highest strains,
In highest worlds be paid,
His glory by our lips proclaim'd,
And by our lives display'd .

5

When shall we reach those blissful realms
Where Christ exalted reigns ;
And learn of the celestial choir
Their own immortal strains .

HYMN IX

On the new YEAR by D.r *Doddridge*   The Mufick by M.r *Selby*

God of my life, thy conftant care, With blefsing crown the Op'ning Year, This guilty life doft thou pro..long, And, wake a..new mine Annual Song.

2

How many kindred fouls are fled,
To the vaft regions of the dead,
Since from this day the changing fun
Thro' his laft yearly period run?

3

We yet furvive but who can fay,
Or thro' the year or month or day,
"I will retain this vital breath;
"Thus far at leaft in league with death?

4

That breath is thine eternal God;
'Tis thine to fix my fouls abode;
It holds its life from thee alone,
On earth or in the world unknown.

5

To thee our fpirits we refign;
Make them and own them ftill as thine;
So fhall they fmile fecure from fear,
Tho' death fhould blaft the rifing year.

On the PASSION   The Mufick by *Mr Selby*

LARGHETTO

From whence thefe dire por_tents, a_round That Earth and Heav'n a__maze. Where.fore do Earthquakes cleave the Ground Why hides the Sun his rays.

2

Not thus did SINAI's trembling head
With facred horror nod,
Beneath the dark pavilion fpread
Of the defcending God!

3

What tongue the tortures can declare
Of this vindictive hour?
Wrath he alone had will to fhare,
As he alone had pow'r!

4

See ftreaming from the fatal tree,
His all atoning blood
Is this the infinite?__Tis He!
My SAVIOUR, and my GOD!

5

For me thefe pangs his foul affail,
For me the death is borne!
My fin gave fharpnefs to the nail,
And pointed ev'ry thorn.

6

Let fin no more my foul enflave;
Break, Lord, the tyrant's chain;
O fave me, whom thou cam'ft to fave,
Nor bleed or die in vain.

HYMN XII

On WHITSUNDAY　　　　by Mr. Dryden　　　　the Mufick by Mr. Selby

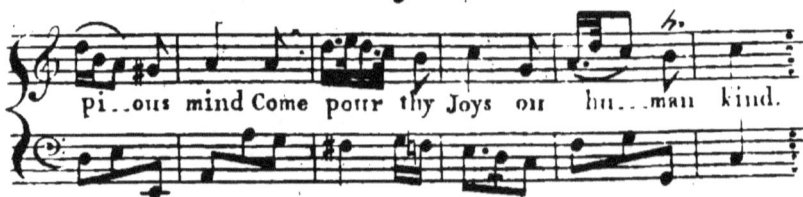

E---ter--nal fpi---rit by whofe Aid The

Worlds foun..da..tions firft were laid Come Vi...fit ev'ry

pi..ous mind Come pourr thy Joys on hu...man kind.

2

From fin and forrow fet us free,
And make thy temples worthy, thee;
Illumine our dull darken'd fight,
Thou fource of uncreated light.

3

Thrice holy fount, thrice holy fire,
Our hearts with heavenly love infpire,
Come and thy facred unction bring,
To fanctify us while we fing.

4

Plenteous of grace defcend from high,
Rich in thy feven fold energy,
Thou ftrength of his almighty hand
Whofe power do'es heaven and earth commands,

5

Proceeding Spirit our defence,
Who doft the gifts of grace difpenfe,
Feeble alas we are and frail,
Let not the world or flefh prevail.

6

Chace from our minds th' infernal foe,
And Peace the fruit of Love beftov:
And left our feet fhould ftep aftray,
Protect and guide us in the way.

7

Make us eternal Truths receive,
And practife all that we believe,
Give us thyfelf that we may fee
The Father and the Son by thee.

8

Immortal honours, endlefs fame
Attend th' Almighty Fathers name,
The Saviour Son be glorified,
Who for loft mans redemption died.

9

And equal adoration be,
Eternal Spirit, paid to thee,
"Come, vifit every pious mind,
"Come pour thy joys on human kind."

Sym This to be play'd only after the laft verfe.

HYMN XIII

On thankfgiving   by Dr DODD   the Mufick by Mr Selby

Glo-ry be to God our King, Thine E-ter-nal love we fing: Thou haft barr'd thine Arm di-vine, Wrought Sal-va-tion; made us thine. Hal.le.lu.jah, Hal.le.lu.jah, Hal.le.lu.jah.

2
Wandering fheep, how far from home
Sore bewilder'd did we roam;
Till the gracious fhepherd came;
Sought, and fav'd: O'praife his name!

3
Death, no more we dread thy fting;
Sin fubdu'd, we joyful fing:
Grave, thy terrors we defy;
We fhall live; for Chrift did die.

4
Fir'd with gratitude, we raife
All our fouls to found thy praife;
Touch each heart, each tongue infpire,
Sing we higher ftill, and higher.

5
Down to deepeft hell depreft,
Jefus refcu'd, rais'd, and bleft;
Open'd mercy's golden gate,
Mercy, here who holds her feat.

6
Happy manfion, every voice,
In the bleft retreat rejoice:
Let each voice united found,
Be the walls with gladnefs crown'd."

7
Elevate our fouls to thee:
Thou our guide and guardian be;
Worthy, worthy may we prove,
Lord, of fuch diftinguifh'd love!

8
Bleffing, thankful all our days,
May we pray, rejoice and praife;
'Till the the glorious trump fhall found,
And our raptur'd hearts rebound. *Hallelujah*

Thanks to GOD.   by Dr. Doddridge   the Musick by Mr. Selby.

All Glo-ri-ous God what hymns of Praise shall

our tran..sport..ed voic...es raise What flam...ing

Love and zeal is due While heav'n stands o...pen to our

View while heav'n stands o...pen to our View

2
Once we were fall'n, and bh how low!
Just on the brink of endless woe:
Doom'd to the heritage of hell;
Where Sinners in deep darkness dwell!

But lo, a ray of chearfull light,
Scatters the horrid Shades of Night:
Lo, what triumphant grace is shewn,
To souls impoverish'd and undone!

4
Far, far beyond these mortal shores
A bright inheritance is ours;
Where saints in light our Coming wait,
To share their holy blissful State.

HYMN XVII

The SINCERE PENITENT   by Mr Lockman

SLOW

Al..migh..ty

_Lord moft mer..ci..full Thefe thanks un..feign'd   thefe

Vows re_ceive Thou who when bath'd in Tears   I

Jay Didft hear my Cries and quick re..lieve   Great

The Mufick by *Dr Arne*

God from all E...ter..ni....ty O may our

Pray'rs af...cend to Thee.

2

Plung'd deep in woe, of hope bereft,
Defruction threaten'd me around;
Remorfe was mine, and black defpair,
And I no ray of comfort found.
Chorus. Great; God &c.

3

For ever, O recorded be
The moment, when thy grace beftow'd
Thro' Chrift, the fight of pard'ning love,
And led me to this bleft abode.
Chorus. Great God, &c.

4

Since treading Virtues facred paths
Alone fecures the mind's content,
May the remainder of my days
In ferving thee be always fpent.
Chorus. Great God from all eternity,
O may our pray'rs afcend to thee.

The

PSALMS and HYMNS

FOR THE

GUITTAR.

The ſpacious Firmament on High,   PSALM **XIX.**

The Lord my Pasture shall prepare,

PSALM XXIII

When all thy Mercies O my God,

HYMN IV

Great God with Wonder and with Praise,   HYMN **V**

Lord of the Sabbath hear us pray   HYMN **VI**

High let us swell our tunefull Notes,   HYMN **VIII**

God of my life thy constant care,   HYMN **IX**

From whence thefe dire portends around,　　　HYMN **X**

Eternal Spirit by whofe Aid,　　　HYMN　**XII**

Glory be to God our King.   HYMN **XIII**

All Glorious God what Hymns of praise,   HYMN **XIV**

Almighty Lord most merciful,   HYMN **XVII**

The PRAYER, *used in the* Magdalen Chapel. *(a)*

FATHER of mercies, and God of all comfort, who has fent thy Son Jefus Chrift into the World, to *feek and to fave that which was loft*; (b) we praife thy holy name for the bountiful provifion made in this place for the fpiritual and temporal wants of miferable offenders: befeeching thee fo to difpofe our Hearts by the powerful influence of thy bleffed Spirit, that thro' fincere repentance and a lively faith, we may obtain remiffion of our fins, and all the *precious promifes* (c) of thy gofpel. Awaken thofe, who have not yet a due fenfe of their guilt; and perfect a godly forrow where it is begun. "Renew in us whatfoever hath been decayed by the fraud and Malice of the Devil, or by *our own carnal will and frailnefs*" (d): Preferve us, *after efcaping the pollufions of the world, from being again intangled therein* (e); and keep us in a ftate of conftant watchfulnefs and humility. Forgive, as we do from our hearts, thofe who have done us wrong; and grant to all, who have feduced others, or been feduced themfelves into wickednefs, that they may forfake the *evil of their doings*, and live. Make this houfe a bleffing, we pray thee, to the fouls and bodies of all its inhabitants; and a glorious monument of thy *grace, abounding to the chief of finners* (f). Strengthen the hands, direct the counfels, reward the labours and the liberality of all who are engaged in the government or fupport of it; and increafe the number of thofe who have a zeal for thy glory, and *compaffion on the ignorant, and on them that are out of the way* (g); that many may be *turned from darknefs to light, and from the power of Satan unto* thee their *God* (h), thro' the merits and mediation of Jefus Chrift our Lord. *Amen.*

(a) This truly Scriptural Prayer, was received into the public Service of the CHAPEL, after having undergone the correction, and obtained the fanction of the late Archbifhop of Canterbury, Dr. SECKER; a generous Friend to the MAGDALEN CHARITY, from the beginning as well as at the End; for he left a handfome legacy to it.
(b) Luke xix. 10.
(c) 2 Pet. i. 4.
(d) See "the order for Vifitation of the Sick," in the Common Prayer Book.
(e) 2 Pet. ii. 20.
(f) 1 Tim. i. 14. 15.
(g) Heb. v. 2.
(h) Acts xxvi. 18.

www.ingramcontent.com/pod-product-compliance
Lightning Source LLC
Chambersburg PA
CBHW021529270326
41930CB00008B/1157